300 (low oven)	150
350 (moderate oven)	175
400 (hot oven)	205
450 (very hot oven)	230
500 (extremely hot oven)	260

LENGTHS

U.S. Measurements	Metric Equivalents
¼ inch	6 mm
½ inch	1.2 cm
¾ inch	2 cm
1 inch	2.5 cm
2 inches	5 cm
5 inches	12.5 cm

LITTLE BOOKS FOR COOKS

TOMATOES

ANDREWS AND MCMEEL

A UNIVERSAL PRESS SYNDICATE COMPANY

KANSAS CITY

ISBN: 0-8362-2781-6
Library of Congress Catalog Card Number: 96-86644

First U.S. edition
1 3 5 7 9 10 8 6 4 2

Editor: Deri Reed
Designer: Yolanda Monteza
Photographer: Steven Mark Needham
Illustrator: Ed Lam

Produced by Smallwood and Stewart, Inc., New York City

TABLE OF CONTENTS

T O M A

Considered an aphrodisiac by some, labeled poisonous by others, and now embraced worldwide, the tomato is an integral part of many cuisines.

The tomato was a staple in Central American villages as long as 5,000 years ago. It probably originated in the Andes, and was domesticated by the ancient peoples of what is now Mexico. In the 16th century, New World explorers took tomato seeds back to Europe. But tomatoes

T O E S

were considered poisonous then and used only ornamentally. Only the Italians embraced the tomato and incorporated it into their cuisine.

Not until the mid-1800s did the rest of Europe—and hence their European descendants in the United States—discover the joys of *eating* the "love apple." Even as late as 1900, there was still some serious debate in the States as to whether tomatoes could be eaten without any ill effects.

Today, we find tomatoes all over the world: In the flavorful red *gazpachos* of Spain, in the spicy hot Mexican *salsas,* as the base for many French stews and roasts, in ketchups and as a sandwich ingredient in America, in Asian chili sauces and, of course, in the ubiquitous Italian tomato sauces.

Is it a fruit or a vegetable? Well, it's both. Botanically, science classifies the tomato as a fruit, but legally—for trade and import purposes—it is a vegetable, thanks to an 1893 Supreme Court decision.

TOMATO NUTRITION

Nutritionally, tomatoes are a good bet: They're loaded with vitamin C, a fair amount of vitamin A, and a good dose of fiber. In addition, they also contain anti-oxidants, which scientists believe may help fight cancer and slow signs of aging.

BUYING AND STORING TOMATOES

When buying fresh tomatoes, look for bright rich color, with no soft spots or blemishes; they should be firm, plump, fully ripe, and heavy for their size.

In the best of all possible worlds, all fresh tomatoes would be vine-ripened—*not* picked when green and then artificially ripened. The flavor and texture are far superior. However, vine-ripened tomatoes can be hard to find (look for them in specialty stores and farmers' markets), and expensive. In winter, when the only fresh tomatoes around are dull, tasteless tomato-wanna-bes, your best bet is to use good canned tomatoes—they'll have a lot more flavor.

The best way to get the freshest, juiciest, most flavorful tomatoes is to grow your own. Tomatoes are easy to cultivate and prolific, so you'll be able to keep all your friends and relatives supplied for the whole of August.

Ripe tomatoes should be stored at room temperature and used within a few days. Never refrigerate or freeze fresh tomatoes (it kills the flavor and texture), although cooked sauces or other dishes made with tomatoes usually freeze very well.

To ripen tomatoes, place them in a paper bag punched with a few holes at room temperature for 2 to 3 days.

GLOBE: Medium-size, firm, and (with luck) juicy — the standard, every-day tomato. Globes are good raw in sandwiches and salads or simply sliced, salted, and served. Cooked, they are an integral part of many sauces and stews.

T O M A T O E S

BEEFSTEAK: Large, deep orange-red, elliptical, very meaty. Beefsteaks are good raw or cooked, and, because of their size, stuffed. They are called beefsteaks because a thick slice looks like a large steak.

PLUM or **ITALIAN PLUM** or **ROMA:** Egg-shaped, red or yellow, available fresh and canned. Plum tomatoes have fewer seeds and can be more flavorful than the larger beefsteaks and globes. Good in sandwiches, salads, sauces, and stews.

YELLOW: Available in different sizes, yellow tomatoes are less acidic and a bit less flavorful than red tomatoes. The yellow cherry tomato makes a novel, attractive garnish.

GREEN (unripe): With a piquant tangy taste, green tomatoes don't have the sweet "tomato-y" flavor of red tomatoes. They are widely available at the end of summer and after the first frost, when unripe tomatoes on the vine must be picked. Green tomatoes are good fried (a Southern classic), combined with red tomatoes in salsas, pickled, or used to add an acidic flavor to soups or stews.

CHERRY: Red or yellow-gold, about 1" diameter. Very fresh-tasting, sweet, and juicy, cherry tomatoes are good in salads or sautéed for a side dish.

OTHER TOMATO PRODUCTS

SUN-DRIED TOMATOES: These tomato halves that are dried in the sun (or by other means) are chewy, dense, and intense in flavor. Sun-dried tomatoes come dry or packed in olive oil; if dry, the tomatoes need to be reconstituted in oil or other liquid before adding to dishes. Use whole or chopped, in salads, soups, sandwiches, and sauces.

CANNED TOMATOES: There are many varieties available, including whole tomatoes in juice or purée, chopped tomatoes, and crushed tomatoes. Use canned tomatoes in sauces and stews when good fresh tomatoes are not available.

TOMATO PASTE: A thick, rich, concentrated sauce made from tomatoes that are cooked a long time, reduced, and strained. Available in cans or tubes. Use to add flavor and body to sauces.

TOMATO PURÉE: Tomatoes are briefly cooked, then puréed and canned. Use to thicken and intensify sauces.

TOMATO SAUCE: Slightly thinner than a purée, with herbs and other flavorings added. Also available are pasta tomato sauces with meat and vegetables.

TOMATO TIPS

To peel tomatoes, make a few shallow inch-long cuts in the skin, submerge in boiling water for 60 seconds, then refresh under cold water; the skin can then be easily peeled off. If you need to peel just one tomato, impale it on a fork and rotate over a gas flame for a minute or so until the skin wrinkles.

To remove seeds from a tomato, slice in half and gently squeeze out the seeds, or put it under running water and scoop out the seeds with your fingers.

Tomatoes that are cut in half vertically (through the core) do not lose as much juice and hold together better than those cut horizontally.

If your stuffed tomatoes won't stand up for cooking, put them in lightly greased muffin tins.

Be sure to wait to add chopped tomatoes to a salad until just before serving—if tomatoes are allowed to sit in a salad, their liquid will dilute the dressing.

RECI

P E S

Gazpacho

What is more refreshing on a hot summer's day than a bowl of chilled gazpacho? If you can, use juicy vine-ripened tomatoes; if they aren't available, a combination of fresh tomatoes and canned gives good results. Try to make this a day ahead, as the gazpacho gains flavor when chilled overnight.

2 pounds fresh ripe tomatoes,
cut into pieces

2 Kirby cucumbers or 1 small cucumber,
peeled and cut into pieces

1 green bell pepper, seeded and
cut into pieces

1/2 small onion, coarsely chopped

2 garlic cloves, chopped

1/4 cup sherry wine vinegar or 5 tablespoons red wine vinegar

2 tablespoons extra virgin olive oil

2 teaspoons sugar

1/4 teaspoon ground cumin

Salt, to taste

Small croutons and finely chopped
tomato, cucumber, and green bell
pepper, for garnish (optional)

In a food processor, combine 1 cup cold water with the tomatoes, cucumbers, pepper, onion, garlic, vinegar, olive oil, sugar, cumin, and salt; process until puréed. Strain into a bowl, pressing with the back of a spoon to extract all the liquid; discard the solids. Adjust the vinegar and salt to taste. Cover and refrigerate several hours or overnight. Garnish the soup as desired just before serving. *Serves 6.*

Light Tomato Sauce

When good fresh tomatoes are available for a quick, light pasta dinner, combine peeled, chopped plum tomatoes, olive oil, parsley, minced garlic, salt, and pepper in a skillet. Stir over medium heat just until heated through, then toss with fresh cooked pasta.

Grilled Baguettes with Fresh Tomato Relish

The success of this simple appetizer depends on using the best-quality ingredients—fresh crusty bread, extra virgin olive oil, and, of course, red ripe tomatoes. It's a good dish to prepare in the late summer, when the reddest, ripest tomatoes are available.

Fresh Tomato Relish:

2 fresh ripe medium globe
      tomatoes, finely chopped

1 small garlic clove, minced

8 fresh basil leaves, minced

1 tablespoon extra virgin olive oil

1/4 teaspoon salt

1/4 teaspoon freshly ground
      black pepper

Grilled Baguettes:

2 tablespoons extra virgin olive oil

1 small garlic clove, crushed

16 slices French bread, about 1/2"
      thick

To prepare the relish, in a medium-size nonreactive bowl, gently toss together the tomatoes, the minced garlic, basil, the 1 tablespoon olive oil, salt, and pepper. Set aside.

To grill the bread, preheat the broiler. In a small skillet, heat the 2 tablespoons olive oil over low heat. Add the crushed garlic, then immediately remove the skillet from the heat and set aside. Arrange the bread slices on an ungreased baking sheet and broil 4" from the heat, on one side only, for 1 to 2 minutes, until golden brown. Remove from the broiler and brush the toasted sides with the garlic oil.

To serve, arrange the bread, toasted side up, on a platter and spoon the tomato relish over them. *Serves 6 to 8.* 🌶️

Stuffed Tomatoes

Cut tomatoes in half vertically and scoop out the seeds and pulp; sprinkle with salt and allow to drain, cut-side down, on paper towels for 15 minutes. Then stuff with tuna, shrimp, or chicken salad for a lunch or brunch entrée.

Green Tomato Salsa

The beauty and sweetness of red tomatoes ripe from the garden is punctuated by the crisp, piquant flavor of a green tomato in this colorful salsa.

2 fresh ripe large red globe
tomatoes, seeded and diced

2 fresh ripe large yellow
tomatoes, seeded and diced

1 fresh medium green tomato,
diced

1 small red onion, diced

1/2 cup minced fresh cilantro

2 tablespoons extra virgin olive oil

2 teaspoons salt

1 teaspoon fresh lime juice

1/2 teaspoon freshly ground black
pepper

1 serrano chile pepper, seeded and
minced (optional)

Place all the ingredients in a large nonreactive bowl and toss to mix thoroughly. Let the mixture sit, covered, at room temperature for 20 to 30 minutes, to allow the flavors to blend. Serve with chips or as a side relish to grilled foods. *Makes about 4 ½ cups.*

Panzanella

In this Italian classic, lush ripe tomatoes are tossed with cool and crunchy cucumbers, sweet red onions, and chunks of bread. Traditionally, the bread is soaked in water, but here we toast olive oil–tossed cubes to a golden crunch. Soaking the raw onion in ice water takes away some of its bite.

1/4 cup thinly sliced onion

1 loaf (10 ounces) semolina bread,
    cut into 1" cubes

3/4 cup olive oil

1/4 cup red wine vinegar

1/2 teaspoon salt

1/4 teaspoon freshly ground black
    pepper

1 garlic clove, halved

1 pound fresh ripe tomatoes, cored
    and cut into 1"-thick wedges

2 medium cucumbers, thinly sliced

2 tablespoons capers, rinsed and
    drained

In a small bowl, combine the onion slices with ice water to cover. Let stand 30 minutes; drain. Meanwhile, preheat the oven to 400°F. In a large bowl, toss the bread cubes with ¼ cup of the olive oil. Spread on a baking sheet and bake for about 7 minutes, until crisp and golden. In a small bowl, combine the remaining ½ cup olive oil, the vinegar, salt, and pepper. Set aside.

Rub a salad bowl with the garlic halves; discard the garlic. In the bowl, combine the onion, bread cubes, tomatoes, cucumbers, and capers. Whisk the olive oil mixture, pour over the salad and toss until well combined. Let stand at least 2 hours at room temperature before serving. *Serves 4.*

Indian Tomato Salad

This refreshing salad, flecked with cumin seeds, is ideal for serving on hot days with grilled and barbecued dishes. To vary the recipe, try substituting finely sliced shallots for the onion or lime juice for the lemon, or add a teaspoon of Dijon mustard to the dressing. Make this salad just before serving.

1/2 teaspoon cumin seeds

1/4 cup extra virgin olive oil

2 tablespoons red wine vinegar

1 tablespoon lemon juice

2 garlic cloves, minced

4 fresh ripe medium globe tomatoes,
    cut into wedges

1 medium onion, thinly sliced

1 small cucumber, thinly sliced

Pinch of freshly ground black pepper

Salt, to taste

5 large mint leaves, finely chopped

Heat a small skillet over medium-high heat. Add the cumin seeds and toast, stirring constantly, 20 to 30 seconds. Transfer to a plate and allow to cool. In a large salad bowl, whisk together the olive oil, vinegar, lemon juice, and garlic. Add the tomatoes, onion, cucumber, pepper, and salt; toss well. Sprinkle with the cumin seeds and mint, toss again, and serve. *Serves 4 to 6.*

Fried Green Tomatoes

To make this Southern classic, dredge ½" green tomato slices in seasoned flour or cornmeal and fry in a nonstick skillet in ½" of 325°F vegetable oil, turning once, until golden brown. Drain on paper towels and serve immediately.

Three-Tomato Salad with Two-Basil Dressing

This salad takes advantage of the explosion of tomato varieties that appear seasonally in specialty produce markets. If you can't find purple basil, use all sweet basil.

Three-Tomato Salad:

3 fresh ripe medium red globe tomatoes

12 fresh ripe yellow pear tomatoes,
     stemmed and cut in half lengthwise

18 fresh ripe red cherry tomatoes,
     stemmed

Two-Basil Dressing:

1 fresh ripe medium red globe tomato,
     peeled, seeded, and chopped

12 fresh sweet basil leaves

12 fresh purple basil leaves

1/4 cup chopped onion

1 teaspoon Dijon mustard

1 teaspoon sugar

2 tablespoons white wine vinegar

1/3 cup extra virgin olive oil

Salt and freshly ground black pepper,
     to taste

To prepare the salad, cut the globe tomatoes into quarters, then cut each quarter into 2 wedges. In a nonreactive bowl, combine all the tomatoes.

To prepare the dressing, in a food processor, combine the chopped globe tomato, 4 leaves of each type of basil, the onion, mustard, sugar, and vinegar; process until puréed. With the motor running, gradually add the olive oil through the feed tube in a thin steady stream until combined. Season with salt and pepper.

Finely shred the remaining basil leaves. Pour the dressing over the tomatoes and toss gently to coat. Add half the shredded basil and toss to combine. Garnish with the remaining shredded basil. *Serves 6 to 8.*

Braised Potatoes with Tomatoes

Potatoes and tomatoes make a delicious pairing thanks to curry-style spices in this hearty dish from India.

3 garlic cloves, halved

One 1" piece fresh ginger root,
   peeled and coarsely chopped

6 tablespoons vegetable oil

1 1/2 cups minced onions

1 medium fresh hot green chile pepper,
   seeded and sliced

1 pound potatoes, peeled and cut
   into 2" pieces

4 fresh ripe medium globe tomatoes,
   cut into quarters

1 teaspoon cumin seeds

1 teaspoon ground cumin

1 teaspoon ground turmeric

1 teaspoon ground coriander

1 teaspoon chili powder

1 teaspoon salt

1/4 cup finely minced fresh cilantro,
   for garnish

In a blender, combine the garlic and ginger; process until finely chopped. Set aside.

In a large saucepan, heat the oil over medium-high heat. Add the onions and cook, stirring occasionally, 10 minutes, until browned. Reduce the heat to medium, add the garlic mixture and the chile, and cook, stirring constantly, 1 minute. Add the potatoes and cook, stirring occasionally, for 5 minutes. Reduce the heat to medium-low and add the tomatoes, cumin seeds, ground cumin, turmeric, coriander, chili powder, and salt. Cook, covered, 20 minutes, until the potatoes are tender. Remove from the heat and garnish with fresh cilantro. *Serves 4.*

Broiled Tomatoes

Halve tomatoes horizontally, season with salt and pepper and dot with butter; broil 4" from heat for 5 minutes, until lightly browned. For added flavor, top with seasoned buttered bread crumbs and grated Parmesan cheese before broiling.

Tomato Mozzarella Salad

For a quick appetizer that takes advantage of peak-of-the-summer succulent tomatoes, arrange tomato and mozzarella slices in an attractive pattern, drizzle with olive oil, scatter with torn fresh basil leaves and chopped red onion, and season generously with salt and pepper.

Summer Tomato Sauce

This is a sauce to make only when tomatoes are at their very best. The vegetables and herbs of summer should allow you to vary this quick, light sauce at will. Try adding peppers, mushrooms, fresh oregano, chile peppers—whatever strikes your fancy. Toss with pasta or serve over grilled summer vegetables, fish, or polenta.

6 tablespoons (3/4 stick) butter

3 pounds fresh ripe plum tomatoes, peeled, seeded, and chopped

1/4 cup minced fresh basil

1 teaspoon salt

1/4 teaspoon freshly ground black pepper

Melt the butter in a large skillet over medium heat. Stir in the tomatoes, basil, salt, and pepper. Simmer for 15 minutes, until slightly thickened.

To store, cool to room temperature, cover and refrigerate for up to 2 weeks. *Serves 6.*

Grilled Tomatoes

Toss cherry tomatoes with olive oil, chopped fresh herbs of your choice, salt, and pepper. Carefully skewer the tomatoes or place them in a grill basket and grill for 4 to 5 minutes, turning once. For larger tomatoes: Cut in half, core, brush with olive oil and grill, cut-side down, 3 to 4 minutes.

Winter Tomato Sauce

This is a savory sauce to make during the months when fresh tomatoes are not available. It's delicious tossed with pasta, but also try it with steamed vegetables. You can vary it by adding chopped fresh fennel, a little citrus rind, or other herbs.

1/4 cup olive oil

2 garlic cloves, minced

1 can (32 ounces) Italian plum
    tomatoes in juice, coarsely
    chopped

1 teaspoon tomato paste

1 teaspoon dried oregano

1 teaspoon salt

1/2 teaspoon freshly ground
    black pepper

In a large skillet, heat the olive oil over medium-high heat; add the garlic and sauté 3 to 4 minutes, until it begins to turn golden. Add the tomatoes with their juice, the tomato paste, oregano, salt, and pepper. Bring to a simmer; cover and simmer 15 minutes more, until thickened. To store, cool to room temperature, cover, and refrigerate for up to 2 weeks. *Serves 6.*

California Winter Pasta

Sweet Italian sausage, artichokes, and olives combine with canned tomatoes for a hearty, homey pasta sauce.

2 tablespoons olive oil

3/4 pound sweet Italian sausage links

3 garlic cloves, minced

1 package (9 ounces) frozen artichoke
    hearts, thawed

1 can (16 ounces) whole tomatoes in
    juice, chopped

Salt and freshly ground black pepper,
    to taste

8 ounces small pitted black olives

1 pound rigatoni

8 ounces Camembert cheese

In a large skillet, heat the olive oil over medium-high heat. Add the sausages and cook, turning occasionally, 5 minutes, until lightly browned on all sides. Add the garlic and cook, stirring frequently, for 2 minutes. Add the artichoke hearts and cook, stirring frequently, for 3 minutes.

Remove the sausages to a cutting board. Reduce the heat to medium and add the tomatoes with their juice. Cut the sausages into ½" slices and return them to the skillet. Cook, stirring occasionally, 5 minutes, until the sauce thickens slightly. Season with salt and pepper. Stir in the olives. Remove the skillet from the heat and keep warm.

Meanwhile, cook the rigatoni in a large pot of boiling water for 8 to 10 minutes, until just tender, or according to package instructions; drain in a colander.

To serve, transfer the rigatoni to a large shallow bowl. Pinch off walnut-size pieces of cheese and add to the pasta. Add the sauce and toss for 30 seconds, until the cheese is melted. Serve immediately. *Serves 6.*

Roasted Chicken with Sun-Dried Tomatoes and Garlic

The intense flavor of sun-dried tomatoes permeates this roasted chicken. Don't let the two heads of garlic frighten you away from this recipe: When roasted, the garlic is sweet and mild.

ROASTED CHICKEN WITH SUN-DRIED
TOMATOES AND GARLIC

12 sun-dried tomatoes (not packed
    in oil)

1 teaspoon minced fresh sage

1 teaspoon fresh rosemary leaves,
    crumbled

1/2 teaspoon freshly ground black
    pepper

One 3- to 3 1/2-pound chicken

1 teaspoon salt

2 teaspoons olive oil

2 garlic heads, cloves separated
    and peeled

In a small saucepan over high heat, combine 2 cups of water with the tomatoes and bring to a boil; boil for 5 minutes. With a slotted spoon, remove the tomatoes, finely chop, and set aside. Boil the tomato liquid for about 10 minutes, until reduced to ¼ cup. Set aside.

In a small bowl, combine the tomatoes, sage, rosemary, and pepper. Using your fingers, gently lift the chicken skin away from the flesh of the breasts and legs; try not to tear the skin. Stuff the tomato mixture under the loosened skin. Sprinkle the chicken cavity with salt. Tie the legs together using kitchen string.

In a large, heavy nonstick saucepan or Dutch oven, heat the olive oil over medium-high heat.

Add the chicken, breast-side down. Scatter the garlic cloves over and around the chicken. Reduce the heat to medium-low and cook, covered, for 20 minutes.

Turn the chicken over and cook, covered, 30 minutes more, until the chicken registers 165°F on a meat thermometer and the juices run clear when a thigh is pierced with a knife. Remove the chicken to a serving platter.

Add the reserved tomato water to the pan and cook, stirring constantly, over high heat for 2 minutes, until thick and slightly syrupy. Spoon the sauce and garlic cloves over the chicken and serve. *Serves 4.*

Slow-Roasted Tomatoes

To give a new life to drab, flavorless tomatoes, try this: Halve the tomatoes, drizzle with olive oil and season with salt and pepper; place in a lightly greased shallow baking pan and bake at 300°F for 2 to 2½ hours, turning occasionally. The slow roasting will bring out and intensify the flavors. Use them in your favorite recipe as you would fresh, or serve as part of an antipasto.

Spicy Shrimp
with Tomatoes

Far East spices spike the fresh tomato sauce in this Indian-flavored shrimp dish. Garam masala, an Indian spice blend, is available in gourmet and Asian food stores.

2 medium onions, chopped

4 garlic cloves, halved

1 medium fresh hot green chile
      pepper, seeded

4 tablespoons vegetable oil

1/2 teaspoon chili powder

1/2 teaspoon ground turmeric

1/2 teaspoon garam masala

4 fresh ripe medium globe tomatoes,
      peeled and sliced

1 pound medium shrimp, shelled
      and deveined

1/2 teaspoon salt

1 tablespoon fresh lemon juice

3 tablespoons finely chopped fresh
      cilantro, for garnish

In a food processor or blender, combine 1 tablespoon of water with the onions, garlic, and chile pepper; process until fine.

In a medium saucepan, heat 3 tablespoons of the oil over high heat. Add the onion mixture and cook, stirring occasionally, 8 minutes, until lightly browned. Reduce the heat to medium, add the chili powder, turmeric, and garam masala, and cook 4 minutes, until all the liquid has evaporated. Reduce the heat to low, add the tomatoes, and cook, covered, 8 to 10 minutes, until the sauce is smooth and thickened.

Meanwhile, in a large nonstick skillet, heat the remaining 1 tablespoon oil over medium-high heat. Add the shrimp and salt and sauté 3 to 5 minutes, until the shrimp turn pink.

Add the shrimp to the tomato sauce and cook, stirring, 1 to 2 minutes more. Sprinkle with the lemon juice and cilantro. *Serves 4.*

WEIGHTS

Ounces and Pounds		Metric Equivalents
½	ounce	14 g
1	ounce	28 g
2	ounces	57 g
4	ounces (¼ pound)	113 g
8	ounces (½ pound)	225 g
16	ounces (1 pound)	454 g

LIQUID MEASURES

tsp.: teaspoon/Tbs.: tablespoon

Spoons and Cups		Metric Equivalents
½	tsp.	2.5 ml
1	tsp.	5 ml
1	Tbs. (3 tsp.)	15 ml
¼	cup	60 ml
⅓	cup	80 ml
½	cup	120 ml
1	cup (8 ounces)	240 ml
4	cups (1 quart)	950 ml
4	quarts (1 gallon)	3.8 liters